The Georgetown Hoyas ™

BY
MARK STEWART

Content Consultant
Matt Zeysing
Historian and Archivist
The Naismith Memorial Basketball Hall of Fame

NORWOODHOUSE PRESS
CHICAGO, ILLINOIS

Norwood House Press
P.O. Box 316598
Chicago, Illinois 60631

For information regarding Norwood House Press, please visit our website at:
www.norwoodhousepress.com or call 866-565-2900.

All photos courtesy of Getty Images except the following:
Basketball Illustrated (6), Collegiate Collection (7, 14, 24, 36 left, 37 left, 41 left),
Condé Nast Publications, Inc. (17), Author's Collection (21, 38, 40), Press Pass Inc. (22), StarPics (23),
Georgetown University/Kids & Cops (25, 36 right, 37 right, 41 top & bottom right), Matt Richman (48),
Associated Press (8, 18, 19, 26, 33, 37 bottom, 39), Icon SMI (15).
Cover Photo: Jim McIsaac/Getty Images

Special thanks to Topps, Inc.

Editor: Mike Kennedy
Designer: Ron Jaffe
Project Management: Black Book Partners, LLC.
Editorial Production: Jessica McCulloch
Research: Joshua Zaffos
Special thanks to Ed Coughlin

Library of Congress Cataloging-in-Publication Data

Stewart, Mark, 1960-
    The Georgetown Hoyas / by Mark Stewart.
       p. cm. -- (Team spirit--college basketball)
    Includes bibliographical references and index.
    Summary: "Presents the history and accomplishments of the Georgetown
University Hoyas basketball team. Includes highlights of players, coaches,
and awards, longstanding rivalries, quotes, timeline, maps, glossary, and
websites"--Provided by publisher.
    ISBN-13: 978-1-59953-364-3 (library edition : alk. paper)
    ISBN-10: 1-59953-364-2 (library edition : alk. paper)
    1. Georgetown Hoyas (Basketball team)--History--Juvenile literature. I.
Title.
    GV885.43.G455S74 2010
    796.323'6309753--dc22
                                        2009033803

Manufactured in the United States of America in North Mankato, Minnesota.
N144—012010

COVER PHOTO: The Hoyas celebrate their 2007 conference championship.

Table of Contents

SPORTS WORDS & VOCABULARY WORDS: In this book, you will find many words that are new to you. You may also see familiar words used in new ways. The glossary on page 46 gives the meanings of basketball words, as well as "everyday" words that have special basketball meanings. These words appear in **bold type** throughout the book. The glossary on page 47 gives the meanings of vocabulary words that are not related to basketball. They appear in ***bold italic type*** throughout the book.

Meet the Hoyas

In the final minutes of a basketball game—when the score is close, the fans are screaming, and the players are exhausted—it takes more than talent and teamwork to win. Sometimes you just have to be a little tougher than your opponent. The Georgetown University basketball team knows this as well as anyone. The Hoyas look for skilled players who work well together and who can dig down for a little extra effort when they need it most.

Georgetown plays in the **Big East Conference**, one of the most competitive in all of sports. Every game is a battle, and every victory is precious. Some years, the Hoyas finish at the top of the **standings** in the Big East. Some years, it takes every ounce of energy to win just a few games in the conference. But make no mistake—Georgetown is always a dangerous opponent.

This book tells the story of the Hoyas. They are famous for finding great centers and for playing hard, physical defense. Win or lose, they bring pride and emotion to the court. This is a big reason why millions of fans across the country think of the Hoyas as their "home" team.

Roy Hibbert and DaJuan Summers leap high to block a shot during a 2006–07 game.

Way Back When

Georgetown played its first basketball game in 1907. But it wasn't until the 1930s that fans around the nation noticed the Hoyas. During that *era*, the team had one of the country's best scorers, Ed Hargaden. He was the school's first **All-American**. The Hoyas also had a great coach in Elmer Ripley.

After Hargaden graduated, the Hoyas struggled to win. Things got so bad that Georgetown planned to give up basketball. That changed when an exciting young guard named Buddy O'Grady joined the team. O'Grady combined with Don Martin and Al Lujack to turn the Hoyas into a confident, winning squad. By the 1941–42 season, Georgetown found itself playing some of the best teams in the country.

A new group of players known as the "Kiddie Korps" took over for the

Hoyas the following season. Dan Kraus dribbled circles around opponents. Billy Hassett's passing and outside shooting were amazing. The team's center, John Mahnken, topped 20 points six times that season—an amazing total in those early days. Georgetown went 19–4 and was invited to play in the championship tournament of the **National Collegiate Athletic Association (NCAA)**. The Hoyas advanced to the championship game but lost to Wyoming, 46–34.

With World War II raging, Georgetown decided to suspend its basketball program. After the war, the Hoyas had to start from scratch on the basketball court. Georgetown struggled for the next 25 years. Jim Barry, a star in the 1960s, was one of the few bright spots for the team.

Finally, in 1972, Georgetown realized it was time to turn the team around. The school hired John Thompson Jr. to coach the Hoyas. He grew up near Georgetown's *campus* and went on to become a famous college player. Later he won two championships with the Boston Celtics of the **National Basketball Association (NBA)**. Thompson was one of the first African-Americans to coach a major college basketball team.

LEFT: John Mahnken defends a shot by superstar center George Mikan.
ABOVE: A trading card of Jim Barry.

Thompson worked hard to maintain Georgetown's high academic standards off the court. He believed that players from all different backgrounds—especially those from the inner cities—could do well at the school. Thompson became an expert at finding stars who also performed well in the classroom. Within 10 years, Georgetown started a new era of success.

Under Thompson, the Hoyas were known for their great talent and *poise*. They were also very good at intimidating opponents. Teams knew to prepare for a battle against Georgetown. Superstars such as Eric "Sleepy" Floyd, Patrick Ewing, Bill Martin, Reggie Williams, and David Wingate made the team one of college basketball's best.

The Hoyas went to the NCAA championship game three times from 1982 to 1985. They won the title in 1984. Thompson was the first African-American coach to accomplish this feat. In the years that followed, Georgetown continued to put great players on the court. A trio of centers—Alonzo Mourning, Dikembe Mutombo, and Othella Harrington—led the way. Other stars in the 1980s and 1990s included Charles Smith, Mark Tillmon, Allen Iverson, Jerome Williams, and Victor Page.

Thompson resigned as coach in 1999. Georgetown had a winning record under him each season for 24 seasons beginning in 1974–75. Hoyas fans hoped for a new era of success as the 21st *century* began.

John Thompson Jr. and Patrick Ewing hug after Georgetown's 1984 national championship.

21st Century

When a school loses a basketball coach like John Thompson Jr., it can take several years for the team to recover. Thompson was replaced by Craig Esherick, who had played for him and was also an assistant coach for the Hoyas. With **power forward** Mike Sweetney leading the way, Georgetown advanced deep in the 2001 **NCAA Tournament**. Two years later, the Hoyas made it to the final game of the **National Invitation Tournament (NIT)**.

Esherick was followed by a coach with a familiar name. John Thompson III—the famous coach's son—took over the Hoyas in 2004–05. "JT3" taught his players a tricky offense based on **team basketball** that drove opponents crazy. Led by young stars like Jeff Green, Roy Hibbert, Tyler Crawford, Jonathan Wallace, and Greg Monroe, Georgetown was unstoppable at times. Another Hoya during this time was Patrick Ewing Jr. Thompson's father had coached Ewing's father 25 years earlier!

In 2006–07, the Hoyas won the Big East and reached the **Final Four** of the NCAA Tournament. It was a thrill for the players and students. For Georgetown's longtime fans, it was just like old times.

John Thompson III gives advice to Roy Hibbert during a 2008–09 game.

Home Court

The Hoyas play their home games in Washington, D.C. Their arena is just a few minutes from campus. It was built in 1997 near the city's Chinatown neighborhood.

Georgetown's arena was called the MCI Center when it opened. After that, its name changed to the Verizon Center. Because MCI and Verizon were both *telecommunications* companies, a lot of fans call the arena the "Phone Booth."

The Hoyas' arena has one of the most amazing high-definition scoreboards in the country. It features four video screens, each one measuring 14 feet high and 25 feet wide. The scoreboard has the ability to show more than 68 billion colors!

BY THE NUMBERS

- *The Hoyas' arena has 20,173 seats for basketball.*
- *The Hoyas share their arena with three **professional** sports teams— the Washington Wizards and Washington Mystics basketball teams, and the Washington Capitals hockey team.*
- *The arena hosted NCAA Tournament games four times from 1998 to 2008.*

Fans fill Georgetown's arena for a 2008–09 game. One of the scoreboard's huge video screens shows the action on the court.

Dressed for Success

The Georgetown uniform is one of the most popular in college basketball. The school's colors of navy blue and gray were chosen long ago to honor the armies of the North and South during the Civil War. In fact, before the team was called the Hoyas, they were known as the Blue & Grey.

Over the years, the Hoyas have experimented with different uniform styles and colors, including black, white, and sky blue. For a few seasons in the 1990s, the home uniform had *HOYAS* spelled out across the front. During most seasons, however, the players have had the school name on their uniforms.

Georgetown®

JOHN DUREN

For more than 80 years, Georgetown's sports teams have gone by the name *Hoyas*. What is a Hoya? It's a Greek word that has been part of a school chant—*Hoya Saxa!*—since the late 1800s. But how the team came to be known as the Hoyas isn't exactly clear. The school newspaper was named *The Hoya*. There was also a dog named Hoya that did tricks for fans at halftime.

John Duren models the Georgetown home uniform from the 1970s.

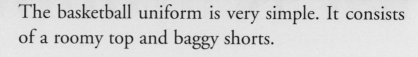

The basketball uniform is very simple. It consists of a roomy top and baggy shorts.

- The top hangs from the shoulders, with big "scoops" for the arms and neck. This style has not changed much over the years.

- Shorts, however, have changed a lot. They used to be very short, so players could move their legs freely. In the last 20 years, shorts have gotten longer and much baggier.

Basketball uniforms look the same as they did long ago … until you look very closely. In the old days, the shorts had belts and buckles. The tops were made of a thick cotton called "jersey," which got very heavy when players sweated. Later, uniforms were made of shiny *satin*. They may have looked great, but they did not "breathe." As a result, players got very hot! Today, most uniforms are made of *synthetic* materials that soak up sweat and keep the body cool.

Jessie Sapp brings the ball up the court in the team's 2008–09 away uniform.

We're Number 1!

No team in sports is truly unbeatable. Georgetown is a perfect example of that. For four incredible seasons in the 1980s, John Thompson Jr.'s Hoyas looked like they could not possibly lose. They reached the NCAA championship game three times but won the title only once. In 1982, it took an amazing shot by Michael Jordan of North Carolina to defeat them. In 1985, the Villanova Wildcats made 90 percent of their shots in the second half—and only beat the Hoyas by two points!

The 1983–84 season, however, belonged to Georgetown from start to finish. The Hoyas didn't just outscore their opponents—they destroyed them. David Wingate was a smooth scorer and a strong leader. Center Patrick Ewing was the best defensive player in the country. Bill Martin helped out Ewing under the backboards. Freshmen Reggie Williams and Michael Graham played with energy and emotion as they gained valuable experience. Michael Jackson showed his toughness by overcoming a painful shoulder injury to lead the team from his position at point guard. And whenever the Hoyas needed fresh troops, Thompson could send anyone on the Georgetown bench into the game, and they got the job done.

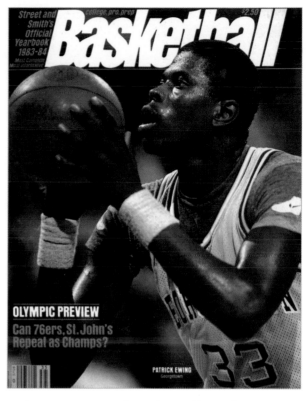

Patrick Ewing appears on the cover of a basketball preview magazine. He was Georgetown's biggest star in 1983–84.

Still, the road to the championship was not an easy one. The Hoyas lost heartbreaking games to Villanova and St. John's during the regular season. In the **Big East Tournament**, they survived a hard battle against Syracuse in the final. And in the second round of the NCAA Tournament, the Hoyas barely won a defensive struggle against Southern Methodist, 37–36.

In its semifinal game against Kentucky, Georgetown faced a tall and talented front line. The Wildcats had a pair of *agile* big men in Sam Bowie and Mel Turpin. Forward Kenny "Sky" Walker was an amazing leaper and an even better scorer. Early in the first half, Ewing was whistled for three fouls. Thompson took him out of the game, and Kentucky raced out to a big lead. The Hoyas were in trouble.

At halftime, Thompson reminded his players that they had already let one championship slip away. They needed to shut down Kentucky in the second half. The players took the court and did exactly as they

were told. Whenever the Wildcats shot, there was a Hoya hand in the
way. Whenever a Kentucky player drove to the basket, two Georgetown
players teamed up to stop him. With the Hoyas hustling all over the
court, the Wildcats made just three shots in the final 20 minutes.
Kentucky scored a grand total of 11 points in the second half, and
Georgetown won 53–40.

The Hoyas faced an even greater challenge in the championship
game. The Houston Cougars shot well, moved fast, and loved to score

on dunks. Fans expected the game to be a contest between Ewing and Hakeem Olajuwon, Houston's star center. Both played well throughout the game, but they were not the difference-makers. Instead, it came down to Houston's excellent starting five against Georgetown's deep and talented **roster**.

Thompson knew his team had an advantage and kept sending fresh players into the game. Slowly but surely, Houston wore down. In the end, the Hoyas were too much for the Cougars. Ewing and Wingate played well on both ends of the court, and Williams and Graham made one big basket after another. The two freshmen shocked Houston with 33 points and 12 rebounds in an 84–75 victory. The Hoyas celebrated the first national championship in school history.

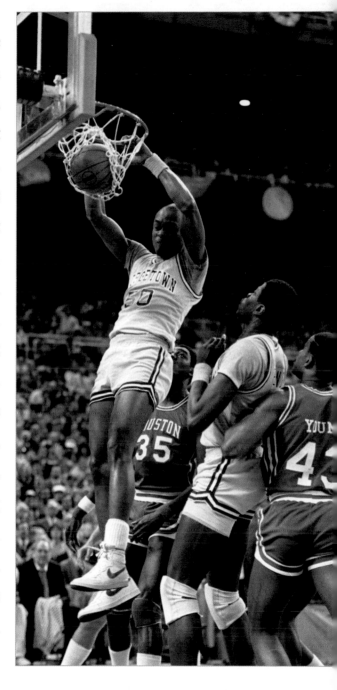

LEFT: The Hoyas celebrate their victory over Kentucky.
RIGHT: Patrick Ewing clears the way for a dunk by Michael Graham against Houston.

Go-To Guys

JOHN DUREN   6′ 3″ Guard

- BORN: 10/30/1958   • PLAYED FOR VARSITY: 1976–77 TO 1979–80

With John Duren playing point guard, Georgetown had a second coach on the floor. He was a great **playmaker** who was famous for keeping his cool in the heat of battle. Duren was named to the **All-Big East** team in 1980 and was the first Hoya to be picked in the first round of the NBA **draft**.

PATRICK EWING   7′ 0″ Center

- BORN: 8/5/1962   • PLAYED FOR VARSITY: 1981–82 TO 1984–85

Patrick Ewing was a ferocious rebounder and shot-blocker who became a very good offensive player. He was named the Big East Defensive Player of the Year in each of his four seasons and won the Naismith Award as the nation's best player in 1985. Ewing was the **Most Outstanding Player (MOP)** in the 1984 NCAA Tournament, when Georgetown won its first championship.

ALONZO MOURNING   6′ 10″ Center

- BORN: 2/8/1970   • PLAYED FOR VARSITY: 1988–89 TO 1991–92

Alonzo Mourning was **recruited** to be a defensive center. He surprised the Hoyas when he arrived with great offensive moves. Mourning's wonderful **all-around** game helped him win Big East Player of the Year in 1992.

OTHELLA HARRINGTON · 6′ 9″ Center

- Born: 1/31/1974 · Played for Varsity: 1992–93 to 1995–96

Othella Harrington teamed with Duane Spencer to give the Hoyas a great one-two punch along the front line. He was Georgetown's leading scorer as a freshman and sophomore. Harrington followed in the footsteps of Patrick Ewing by being named Big East **Rookie of the Year**.

ALLEN IVERSON · 6′ 0″ Guard

- Born: 6/7/1975 · Played for Varsity: 1994–95 to 1995–96

Allen Iverson only played two years for the Hoyas before jumping to the NBA, but those seasons were unforgettable. He scored more than 1,500 points and dazzled fans with his explosive skills and fearless play. Iverson was named Big East Rookic of the Year in 1995 and an All-American in 1996.

JEFF GREEN · 6′ 9″ Forward

- Born: 8/28/1986
- Played for Varsity: 2004–05 to 2006–07

Jeff Green was a born leader. John Thompson III called him the smartest player he ever coached. Green was named Big East Player of the Year in 2007. That March, he led the Hoyas to the Final Four with a great victory over top-ranked North Carolina.

A photo signed by Jeff Green after Georgetown's win over North Carolina in 2007.

JOHN MAHNKEN   6′ 8″ Center

• BORN: 6/16/1922   • DIED: 12/14/2000   • PLAYED FOR VARSITY: 1942–43

John Mahnken's college career was cut short because he served in World War II. But he made his mark in the 27 games he played. Mahnken was a threat to score 20 points or more every time he stepped on the court. In 1943, he became the first Hoya to be named a First Team All-American.

JIM BARRY   6′ 6″ Forward

• BORN: 7/4/1943   • PLAYED FOR VARSITY: 1962–63 TO 1965–66

Jim Barry was nicknamed "Boo" because he surprised opponents by swishing shots from all over the court. He scored 29 points in his first game and averaged 22.6 points for the season. Knee injuries kept Barry from becoming a superstar—but not from winning the Daly Award twice as Georgetown's **Most Valuable Player (MVP)**.

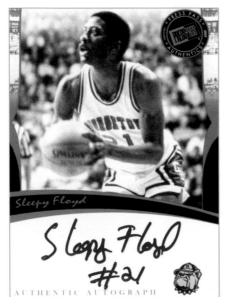

SLEEPY FLOYD   6′ 3″ Guard

• BORN: 3/6/1960

• PLAYED FOR VARSITY: 1978–79 TO 1981–82

When Sleepy Floyd got hot, no one could stop him. He was a sensational athlete, **clutch** scorer, and popular team leader. Floyd was a master at slicing through the defense and swishing baskets from 15 to 18 feet. He led the Hoyas in scoring four years in a row and graduated with the school record for points.

REGGIE WILLIAMS   6′ 7″ Forward

• BORN: 3/5/1964   • PLAYED FOR VARSITY: 1983–84 TO 1986–87

Reggie Williams had an accurate jump shot and a quick first step to the basket. He used both to lead the Hoyas in scoring as a senior with 23.6 points a game. Williams was one of four Georgetown players to score 2,000 points in his career.

VICTOR PAGE   6′ 4″ Guard

• BORN: 2/19/1975

• PLAYED FOR VARSITY: 1995–96 TO 1996–97

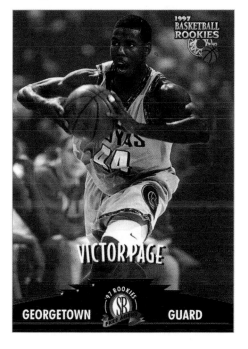

During their one year together, Victor Page and Allen Iverson were one of the most fantastic scoring duos in school history. The following season, when Iverson jumped to the NBA, Page took charge of the offense by himself. Page and Iverson were the only Hoyas to leave school early while John Thompson Jr. was the coach.

MIKE SWEETNEY   6′ 8″ Forward

• BORN: 10/25/1982   • PLAYED FOR VARSITY: 2000–01 TO 2002–03

Mike Sweetney was a classic college power forward. He could muscle his way to the basket for easy shots and fight off big centers for rebounds. He led the Hoyas in scoring in each of his three seasons. Sweetney's 776 points in 2002–03 were the third-highest total in school history.

LEFT: Sleepy Floyd   **ABOVE**: Victor Page

MERLIN WILSON   6′ 9″ Center

Georgetown®

MERLIN WILSON

- BORN: 12/6/1956
- PLAYED FOR VARSITY: 1972–73 TO 1975–76

Whenever a shot clanked off the rim, Merlin Wilson believed the rebound was his. He was the first star recruited by John Thompson Jr., and the first of Georgetown's great big men. Wilson graduated with more than 1,200 rebounds, including eight 20-rebound games.

DERRICK JACKSON   6′ 1″ Guard

- BORN: 8/8/1956
- PLAYED FOR VARSITY: 1974–75 TO 1977–78

Derrick Jackson made a buzzer-beater in 1975 that sent Georgetown to the NCAA Tournament for the first time in more than 30 years. Jackson was just a freshman that season, but he had the *composure* of a *veteran*. He led the Hoyas in points as a sophomore, junior, and senior, and graduated as the school's all-time leading scorer.

CRAIG SHELTON   6′ 7″ Forward

- BORN: 5/1/1957   • PLAYED FOR VARSITY: 1976–77 TO 1979–80

Craig Shelton had a knack for taking over big games. He made key shots in some of Georgetown's greatest victories. Shelton was named to the All-Big East team in 1980. He graduated that year with more points than all but two other Hoyas.

MICHAEL JACKSON   6′ 2″ Guard

- BORN: 7/13/1964
- PLAYED FOR VARSITY: 1982–83 TO 1985–86

When the Hoyas needed leadership on the court, they looked to Michael Jackson. When they desperately needed a basket, they looked to Jackson, too. His fantastic performance during the 1984 Final Four was a key in Georgetown's two great wins.

1985-86 HOYAS

30 Michael Jackson
Guard
6′2′′
Senior
Reston, VA

Michael Jackson

DAVID WINGATE   6′ 5″ Forward

- BORN: 12/15/1963
- PLAYED FOR VARSITY: 1982–83 TO 1985–86

David Wingate was Georgetown's "stopper"—he specialized in guarding the other team's best player. He also had good offensive moves and a reliable outside shot. In the 1984 NCAA Tournament, he was the team's second-leading scorer.

DIKEMBE MUTOMBO   7′ 2″ Center

- BORN: 6/25/1966   • PLAYED FOR VARSITY: 1988–89 TO 1990–91

Few college players have ever ruled the court the way Dikembe Mutombo did. He used his long arms and quick reflexes to swat any shot near the basket. In the first game of his senior season, Mutombo had an amazing **triple-double**: 32 points, 21 rebounds, and 11 blocked shots.

LEFT: Merlin Wilson   **ABOVE**: Michael Jackson

On the Sidelines

Georgetown has had some of the smartest coaches in basketball history. During the 1940s, Elmer Ripley led the Hoyas to the NCAA championship game. Twenty years earlier, Ripley had been one of the top players in professional basketball. After leaving Georgetown, he coached the Harlem Globetrotters, as well as the Canadian and Israeli teams in the *Olympics*.

During the 1950s, another all-time great star coached the team. Buddy Jeannette was known for his attacking offense and tough defense as a player. Under Jeannette, the Hoyas played the same way.

Georgetown basketball reached new heights after John Thompson Jr. was hired to coach the team. During his NBA career, Thompson was a valuable **role player**. This helped him understand the importance of having a deep and *versatile* **lineup**, which would become a trademark of Georgetown's most successful teams.

Thompson built his teams around smart and talented stars. Georgetown offered a fantastic education, and he made sure his players earned their diplomas. Basketball stardom, Thompson insisted, might only last a few years. A Georgetown education would last a lifetime.

John Thompson Jr. hugs his son, John Thompson III, after a big win. Thompson III followed his dad and became the coach of the Hoyas.

27

Rivals

During the early years of the 20th century, Georgetown's sports *rivals* included schools such as Columbia, Princeton, and Yale. When the Big East Conference was formed in 1979, the Hoyas found themselves going nose-to-nose with a group of new teams.

During the 1980s, Georgetown and St. John's ruled the Big East. Patrick Ewing and the Hoyas loved to do battle with Chris Mullin and the Redmen (now the Red Storm). Every meeting between the schools felt like a championship game.

Georgetown fans can usually expect a tough game against St. John's. The teams face off once a year—and maybe a second time if both make the Big East Tournament. For fans of the Hoyas, sometimes the season hasn't been a true success unless they've beaten the Red Storm at least once.

Today, Georgetown's main basketball rival is Syracuse. The rivalry became heated in 1980, when the Hoyas staged a great *comeback* in the final game in Syracuse's old Manley Field House. Afterward, coach John Thompson Jr. grabbed the arena's microphone and shouted to the students that their building was "officially closed!" Georgetown's victory that day ended the Orangemen's 57-game winning streak at home.

Dikembe Mutombo blocks a shot by Syracuse's Billy Owens.

The Hoyas and Orangemen have had some memorable battles in Syracuse's new arena, the Carrier Dome. Crowds there often swell to more than 30,000! Over the years, Georgetown has enjoyed playing in the Carrier Dome. But nothing feels quite as satisfying as beating Syracuse.

One Great Day

When Georgetown hosted Duke in January of 2006, no one expected the Hoyas to put up much of a fight. The Blue Devils were off to a 17–0 start—the best in school history. They were the nation's top-ranked team, while Georgetown wasn't ranked at all. To make matters worse, the Hoyas hadn't beaten a ranked team in their last nine tries. Coach John Thompson III believed the Hoyas had a chance, but they would have to follow his game plan to perfection.

Much of what Thompson knew about coaching came from his days as an assistant and head coach at Princeton. Those teams scored many amazing victories by playing "old-time" ball. They set **picks** and surprised opponents with quick fakes and sneaky cuts to the basket.

A sellout crowd cheered the Hoyas as they out-hustled the Blue Devils for layups and tip-ins. Meanwhile, Georgetown kept Duke from scoring with good defense and rebounding. The Hoyas took control of the game midway through the first half when they made five baskets in a row.

Georgetown fans spill onto the court after the team's
amazing victory over Duke.

Georgetown led by 16 points in the second half, but Duke came
roaring back. J.J. Redick began hitting long jump shots for the Blue
Devils. But Jeff Green, Darrel Owens, and Brandon Bowman answered
for the Hoyas. They combined for 54 points. The Blue Devils had a
chance to tie the game in the final moments, but Jonathan Wallace
stole the ball for the Hoyas. Georgetown won 87–84.

Hundreds of people streamed onto the court when the final buzzer
sounded. Among them was John Thompson Jr., the proudest father in
Washington that day. He gave his son a bear hug.

"That's my child," Thompson shouted. "I love my child!"

It Really Happened

During the mid-1980s, nothing could match the *intensity* of a Georgetown–St. John's basketball game. The Hoyas and Redmen had two of the best teams in the country. Early in 1985, St. John's beat Georgetown in Washington, 66–65. That ended a 29-game winning streak by the Hoyas. Lou Carnesecca, the coach of the Redmen, was famous for his ugly sweaters. The one he wore to this game was horrible—muddy brown with red and blue-green stripes. After beating Georgetown, he kept wearing it game after game.

The teams met again in February. They played in New York's Madison Square Garden, which was a short subway ride from the St. John's campus. Fans of both teams were very tense as they entered the building. The players were on edge during warm-ups. Carnesecca moved nervously along the sideline. Georgetown coach John Thompson Jr. was normally super-serious in these situations. But as he walked onto the court, a smile crept across his face.

Thompson opened his jacket to reveal an exact copy of Carnesecca's sweater. The fans started pointing. The Georgetown players started grinning. Even the referees had to laugh.

By the time the game started, the Hoyas were relaxed and confident. They defeated the Redmen easily, 85–69. Reggie Williams

Seeing Lou Carnesecca dressed in a sweater like this one gave John Thompson Jr. the idea to copy his friend and opponent.

scored 25 points, and Patrick Ewing added 20. Georgetown went on to beat St. John's twice more in the following weeks—first in the Big East championship game and again in the Final Four of the NCAA Tournament. To this day, fans claim that the team's success all started with the famous "Sweater Game."

Team Spirit

Since there is no such thing as a Hoya, Georgetown students decided long ago to make their *mascot* a dog. One of the most famous was Stubby. He was a terrier who was awarded a medal for his heroism during World War I.

During the 1960s, the school's sports teams began using a *logo* of a cartoon bulldog with a blue and gray cap. In the 1970s, Jack the Bulldog became the team's mascot. Jack is actually played by a student in a furry blue and gray costume. Georgetown was one of the first schools to use a "human" mascot. In the 1990s, the Hoyas also started using a live bulldog as a mascot, which they had done several times before.

Another Georgetown *tradition* is its wacky fight song. It was written many years ago and is actually a combination of several songs. It pokes fun at the fight songs of some of the colleges Georgetown plays. The words are almost impossible to remember. At the end of the song everyone shouts, "Hoya Saxa!" That chant actually mixes a Greek word (hoya) with a Latin word (saxa). It means "What Rocks" and celebrates Georgetown's rock-solid sports teams.

Roy Hibbert celebrates with Georgetown fans after a victory during the 2005–06 season.

Timeline

The basketball season is played from October through March. That means each season takes place at the end of one year and the beginning of the next. In this timeline, the accomplishments of the team are shown by season.

1906–07
Georgetown wins its first basketball game.

1954–55
Dale Smith sets a team record with 29 rebounds in a game.

1979–80
John Duren is named Big East Player of the Year.

1942–43
The Hoyas reach the final game of the NCAA Tournament.

1949–50
Tom O'Keefe is the first Hoya to score 1,000 points.

1972–73
John Thompson Jr. is hired as head coach.

Georgetown

Tom O'Keefe

TOM O'KEEFE

1985-86 HOYAS

John Thompson Jr.

Coach John Thompson
1985 NABC Coach of the Year

Georgetown

REGGIE WILLIAMS

Reggie Williams,
a star for the
1984 champs.

Dikembe
Mutombo

1988-89 HOYAS

55 Dikembe Mutombo
6'11''   Sophomore
Center   Kinshasa, Zaire

1983–84
The Hoyas win
the national
championship.

1988–89
Dikembe
Mutombo blocks
12 shots in a game.

2008–09
Greg Monroe is
named Big East
Rookie of the Year.

1980–81
Fred Brown is
named Big East
Freshman of the Year.

2001–02
Kevin Braswell sets
the career record
for **assists**.

2006–07
The Hoyas return
to the Final Four.

The Hoyas
celebrate
in 2007.

37

Fun Facts

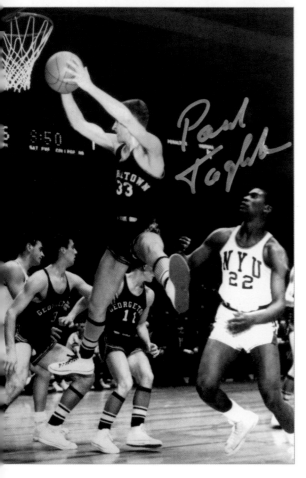

SECOND SPORT

One of the Hoyas' best players during the 1960s was Paul Tagliabue. In 1989, Tagliabue became commissioner of the *National Football League (NFL)*.

FOUR-LETTER GUY

In 1995–96, a freshman named Dean Berry tried out for the Hoyas and made the team. He was a key player for four years, winning a varsity letter each season. Berry was the first **walk-on** in school history to earn four letters.

LITTLE BIG MAN

In 1987–88, Perry McDonald led the Hoyas with 6.3 rebounds per game. McDonald was the only guard in team history to finish a season as the rebounding champion.

ABOVE: An autographed photo of Paul Tagliabue.
RIGHT: Patrick Ewing and Alonzo Mourning

CENTER PIECES

Georgetown centers stick together. When Alonzo Mourning learned that he needed a kidney transplant, Patrick Ewing offered one of his. Ewing wasn't a match—luckily Mourning's cousin was, and the transplant was a success.

STOLEN MOMENTS

Defense has always been the name of the game for Georgetown. The Hoya who made the most steals in his career was Kevin Braswell. He had 349. Allen Iverson holds the records for steals in a season (124) and a game (10).

SHORT CHANGED

When Dikembe Mutombo joined the Hoyas in 1988, opponents were hardly expecting a giant shot-blocker. A scouting guide had mistakenly printed his height as 5′ 10″ instead of 7′ 2″.

BOMBS AWAY

The Hoyas set a school record by making seventeen 3-pointers against Villanova during the 2008 Big East Tournament.

For the Record

The great Georgetown teams and players have left their marks on the record books. These are the "best of the best" …

HOYAS AWARD WINNERS

DEFENSIVE PLAYER OF THE YEAR

Alonzo Mourning	1991–92

NCAA TOURNAMENT MOP

Patrick Ewing	1983–84

BIG EAST FRESHMAN/ROOKIE OF THE YEAR**

Fred Brown	1980–81
Patrick Ewing	1981–82
Othella Harrington	1992–93
Allen Iverson	1994–95
Jeff Green*	2004–05
Greg Monroe	2008–09

NAISMITH AWARD

Patrick Ewing	1984–85

Shared this honor with another player.
**Award was renamed in 1989–90.*

BIG EAST TOURNAMENT MVP

Craig Shelton	1979–80
Sleepy Floyd	1981–82
Patrick Ewing	1983–84
Patrick Ewing	1984–85
Reggie Williams	1986–87
Charles Smith	1988–89
Alonzo Mourning	1991–92
Victor Page	1995–96
Jeff Green	2006–07

BIG EAST PLAYER OF THE YEAR

John Duren	1979–80
Patrick Ewing*	1983–84
Patrick Ewing*	1984–85
Reggie Williams	1986–87
Charles Smith	1988–89
Alonzo Mourning	1991–92
Jeff Green	2006–07

A pennant from Georgetown's early days, before the school's mascot was a bulldog.

HOYAS ACHIEVEMENTS

ACHIEVEMENT	YEAR
NCAA Finalists	1942–43
Big East Tournament Champions	1979–80
Big East Tournament Champions	1981–82
NCAA Finalists	1981–82
Big East Tournament Champions	1983–84
NCAA Champions	1983–84
Big East Tournament Champions	1984–85
NCAA Finalists	1984–85
Big East Tournament Champions	1986–87
Big East Tournament Champions	1988–89
NIT Finalists	1992–93
NIT Finalists	2002 03
Big East Tournament Champions	2006–07

1988-89 HOYAS

33 Alonzo Mourning
6'10''   Freshman
Center   Chesapeake, VA.

TOP RIGHT: Alonzo Mourning, the 1992 Defensive Player of the Year.
BOTTOM RIGHT: Fred Brown, the 1981 Big East Rookie of the Year.
BELOW: Patrick Ewing, the leader of the 1984 champs.

Georgetown

PATRICK EWING

HOYA MOTION!

The Big East

T he Hoyas are part of the Big East. Georgetown was one of seven schools that formed the conference in 1979. Since then the Big East has grown to 16 schools. These are the Hoyas' neighbors …

THE BIG EAST

1. Syracuse University Orange
   Syracuse, New York
2. University of Louisville Cardinals
   Louisville, Kentucky
3. Marquette University Golden Eagles
   Milwaukee, Wisconsin
4. University of Connecticut Huskies
   Storrs, Connecticut
5. University of Pittsburgh Panthers
   Pittsburgh, Pennsylvania
6. Villanova University Wildcats
   Villanova, Pennsylvania
7. DePaul University Blue Demons
   Chicago, Illinois
8. Georgetown University Hoyas
   Washington, D.C.
9. West Virginia University Mountaineers
   Morgantown, West Virginia
10. University of Notre Dame Fighting Irish
    South Bend, Indiana
11. University of Cincinnati Bearcats
    Cincinnati, Ohio
12. Providence College Friars
    Providence, Rhode Island
13. St. John's University Red Storm
    Queens, New York
14. Seton Hall University Pirates
    South Orange, New Jersey
15. Rutgers University Scarlet Knights
    New Brunswick, New Jersey
16. University of South Florida Bulls
    Tampa, Florida

The College Game

Collegebasketball may look like the same game you see professional teams play, but there are some important differences. The first is that college teams play half as many games as the pros do. That's because the players have to attend classes, write papers, and study for exams! Below are several other differences between college and pro basketball.

CLASS NOTES

Most college players are younger than pro players. They are student-athletes who have graduated from high school and now play on their school's varsity team, which is the highest level of competition. Most are between the ages of 18 and 22.

College players are allowed to compete for four seasons. Each year is given a different name or "class"—freshman (first year), sophomore (second year), junior (third year), and senior (fourth year). Sometimes highly skilled players leave college before graduation to play in the pros.

RULE BOOK

There are several differences between the rules in college basketball and the NBA. Here are the most important ones: 1) In college, games last 40 minutes. Teams play two 20-minute halves. In the pros, teams play 48-minute games, divided into four 12-minute quarters. 2) In college, players are disqualified after five personal fouls. In the pros, that number is six. 3) In college, the 3-point line is 20′ 9″ from the basket. In the pros, the line is three feet farther away.

WHO'S NUMBER 1?

How is the national championship of basketball decided? At the end of each season, the top teams are invited to play in the NCAA Tournament. The teams are divided into four groups, and the winner of each group advances to the Final Four. The Final Four consists of two semifinal games. The winners then play for the championship of college basketball.

CONFERENCE CALL

College basketball teams are members of athletic conferences. Each conference represents a different part of the country. For example, the Atlantic Coast Conference is made up of teams from up and down the East Coast. Teams that belong to the same conference usually play each other twice—once on each school's home court. Teams also play games outside their conference. Wins and losses in these games do not count in the conference standings. However, they are very important to a team's national ranking.

TOURNAMENT TIME

At the end of the year, most conferences hold a championship tournament. A team can have a poor record and still be invited to play in the NCAA Tournament if it wins the conference tournament. For many schools, this is an exciting "second chance." In most cases, the regular-season winner and conference tournament winner are given spots in the national tournament. The rest of the tournament "bids" are given to the best remaining teams.

Glossary

ALL-AMERICAN—A college player voted as the best at his position.

ALL-AROUND—Good at all parts of the game.

ALL-BIG EAST—An honor given each year to the conference's best players at each position.

ASSISTS—Passes that lead to successful shots.

BIG EAST CONFERENCE—A conference originally created for teams in the Northeast. It has expanded to include teams from the Southeast and Midwest. The Big East began play in 1979.

BIG EAST TOURNAMENT—The competition that decides the champion of the conference.

CLUTCH—Able to perform well under pressure.

DRAFT—The annual meeting during which NBA teams choose from a group of the best college players. The draft is held each summer.

FINAL FOUR—The term for the last four teams remaining in the NCAA Tournament.

LINEUP—The list of players who are playing in a game.

MOST OUTSTANDING PLAYER (MOP)—The award given each year to the best player in the NCAA Tournament.

MOST VALUABLE PLAYER (MVP)—The award given each year to a team's best player; also given to the best player in a conference.

NATIONAL BASKETBALL ASSOCIATION (NBA)—The professional league that has been operating since 1946–47.

NATIONAL COLLEGIATE ATHLETIC ASSOCIATION (NCAA)—The organization that oversees the majority of college sports.

NATIONAL INVITATION TOURNAMENT (NIT)—The competition that used to determine the champion of college basketball. The NIT began in 1938. Today, there is a preseason and postseason NIT.

NCAA TOURNAMENT—The competition that determines the champion of college basketball.

PICKS—Ways that a player can help a teammate get open by using his body to block the defender guarding him.

PLAYMAKER—Someone who helps his teammates score by passing the ball.

POWER FORWARD—The bigger and stronger of a team's two forwards.

PROFESSIONAL—A player or team that plays a sport for money. College players are not paid, so they are considered "amateurs."

RECRUITED—Offered an athletic scholarship to a prospective student. College teams compete for the best high school players every year.

ROLE PLAYER—A player who is asked to do specific things when he is in a game.

ROOKIE OF THE YEAR—The annual award given to a league's best first-year player.

ROSTER—The list of players on a team.

STANDINGS—A daily list of teams, starting with the team with the best record and ending with the team with the worst record.

TEAM BASKETBALL—A style of play that involves everyone on the court instead of just one or two stars.

TRIPLE-DOUBLE—A game in which a player records double-figures in three different statistical categories.

WALK-ON—A player who earns a spot on a college team without being awarded a scholarship.

OTHER WORDS TO KNOW

AGILE—Quick and graceful.

CAMPUS—The grounds and buildings of a college.

CENTURY—A period of 100 years.

COMEBACK—The process of catching up from behind, or making up a large deficit.

COMPOSURE—A feeling of calm and confidence.

ERA—A period of time in history.

INTENSITY—Strength and energy.

LOGO—A symbol or design that represents a company or team.

MASCOT—An animal or person believed to bring a group good luck.

NATIONAL FOOTBALL LEAGUE (NFL)—The league that started in 1920 and is still operating today.

OLYMPICS—An international sports competition held every four years.

POISE—Calm and confident.

RIVALS—Extremely emotional competitors.

SATIN—A smooth, shiny fabric.

SYNTHETIC—Made in a laboratory, not in nature.

TELECOMMUNICATIONS—Technology that deals with different forms of communication, such as phones.

TRADITION—A belief or custom that is handed down from generation to generation.

VERSATILE—Able to do many things well.

VETERAN—A player with many years of experience.

Places to Go

ON THE ROAD

GEORGETOWN HOYAS
601 F Street, NW
Washington, D.C. 20004
(202) 687-2492

NAISMITH MEMORIAL BASKETBALL HALL OF FAME
1000 West Columbus Avenue
Springfield, Massachusetts 01105
(877) 4HOOPLA

ON THE WEB

THE GEORGETOWN HOYAS   guhoyas.cstv.com
  • *Learn more about the Hoyas*

BIG EAST CONFERENCE   www.bigeast.org
  • *Learn more about the Big East Conference teams*

THE BASKETBALL HALL OF FAME   www.hoophall.com
  • *Learn more about history's greatest players*

ON THE BOOKSHELF

To learn more about the sport of basketball, look for these books at your library or bookstore:
  • Labrecque, Ellen. *Basketball*. Ann Arbor, Michigan: Cherry Lake Publishing, 2009.
  • Porterfield, Jason. *Basketball in the Big East Conference*. New York, New York: Rosen Central, 2008.
  • Stewart, Mark and Kennedy, Mike. *Swish: the Quest for Basketball's Perfect Shot*. Minneapolis, Minnesota: Millbrook Press, 2009.

Index

About the Author

MARK STEWART has written more than 30 books on basketball players and teams, and over 100 sports books for kids. He has also interviewed dozens of athletes, politicians, and celebrities. Mark grew up in New York City and was a fan of the NBA's New York Knicks. He was thrilled when Patrick Ewing joined the team. He later got to meet the great Georgetown center. Mark comes from a family of writers. His grandfather was Sunday Editor of *The New York Time*s and his mother was Articles Editor for *Ladies' Home Journal* and *McCall's*. Mark became interested in sports during lazy summer days spent at the Connecticut home of his father's godfather, sportswriter John R. Tunis. Mark is a graduate of Duke University, with a degree in History. He lives with his wife Sarah, and daughters Mariah and Rachel, overlooking Sandy Hook, New Jersey.

MATT ZEYSING is the resident historian at the Basketball Hall of Fame in Springfield, Massachusetts. His research interests include the origins of the game of basketball, the development of professional basketball in the first half of the 20th century, and the culture and meaning of basketball in American society.